Pebble® Plus

Plant Parts
Seeds

by Vijaya Khisty Bodach

Consulting Editor: Gail Saunders-Smith, PhD

Consultant: Judson R. Scott, Current President
American Society of Consulting Arborists

Capstone
press®

Mankato, Minnesota

Pebble Plus is published by Capstone Press,
151 Good Counsel Drive, P.O. Box 669, Mankato, Minnesota 56002.
www.capstonepub.com

Books published by Capstone Press are manufactured with paper
containing at least 10 percent post-consumer waste.

Library of Congress Cataloging-in-Publication Data
Bodach, Vijaya Khisty.
    Seeds / by Vijaya Khisty Bodach.
    p. cm.—(Pebble plus. Plant parts)
    Summary: "Simple text and photographs present the seeds of plants, how they grow, and their
uses"—Provided by publisher.
    Includes bibliographical references and index.
    ISBN-13: 978-0-7368-6346-9 (hardcover)
    ISBN-10: 0-7368-6346-X (hardcover)
    ISBN-13: 978-0-7368-9623-8 (softcover pbk.)
    ISBN-10: 0-7368-9623-6 (softcover pbk.)
    1. Seeds—Juvenile literature. I. Title. II. Series.
QK661.B63 2007
575.6'8—dc22   2006000994

Editorial Credits
Sarah L. Schuette, editor; Jennifer Bergstrom, designer; Kelly Garvin, photo researcher/photo editor

Photo Credits
Capstone Press/Karon Dubke, cover, 1
Dwight R. Kuhn, 7, 12–13, 20–21, 22 (all)
Getty Images Inc./Taxi/Roger Spooner, 15
Peter Arnold/Manfred Danegger, 10–11
Robert McCaw, 18–19
Shutterstock/iwka, 17; Steve McWilliam, 8–9; Thomas Mounsey, 4–5

Note to Parents and Teachers

The Plant Parts set supports national science standards related to identifying plant
parts and the diversity and interdependence of life. This book describes and illustrates
seeds. The images support early readers in understanding the text. The repetition of
words and phrases helps early readers learn new words. This book also introduces early
readers to subject-specific vocabulary words, which are defined in the Glossary section.
Early readers may need assistance to read some words and to use the Table of Contents,
Glossary, Read More, Internet Sites, and Index sections of the book.

Printed in the United States of America in North Mankato, Minnesota.
032011   006118R

Table of Contents

Plants Need Seeds. 4

Spreading Seeds 10

Seeds We Eat 16

Wonderful Seeds 20

Parts of a Pea Plant 22

Glossary 23

Read More 23

Index 24

Internet Sites. 24

Plants Need Seeds

Plants make seeds.

Each seed can grow

into a new plant.

5

Seeds need soil, water,

and warmth to grow.

Seeds break open in soil.

Stems grow up.

Roots grow down.

The new plant makes leaves,
flowers, and fruit.
Seeds grow inside the fruit.

Spreading Seeds

Birds help spread seeds
when they eat berries.
The seeds come out
in their waste
and fall to the ground.

Weather spreads seeds.

Dandelion seeds float

to new places with the wind.

People scatter seeds.
Pumpkin seeds grow well
in large gardens.

Seeds We Eat

Many seeds are good to eat.

Peas are soft seeds

that grow in pods.

Sunflower seeds

make crunchy snacks.

These hard seeds grow

in the middle of sunflowers.

19

Wonderful Seeds

Large or small, hard or soft,

seeds grow into new plants.

Parts of a Pea Plant

leaves

pod

stem

seed

roots

flower

Glossary

root—the parts of a plant that grow mostly underground; roots take in water and food from the soil.

soil—the dirt where plants grow; most plants get their food and water from the soil.

stem—the long main parts of a plant that makes leaves; food gathered by roots moves through stems to the rest of the plant.

waste—the part of food that isn't used by the body; people and animals get rid of waste.

Read More

Branigan, Carrie, and Richard Dunne. *Flowers and Seeds.* World of Plants. North Mankato, Minn.: Smart Apple Media, 2005.

Farndon, John. *Seeds.* World of Plants. San Diego: Blackbirch Press, 2005.

Mattern, Joanne. *How Peas Grow.* How Plants Grow. Milwaukee: Weekly Reader, 2006.

Index

berries, 10

birds, 10

fruit, 8

leaves, 8

peas, 16

people, 14

pumpkin seeds, 14

roots, 6

soil, 6

stems, 6

sunflowers, 18

weather, 12

Word Count: 124
Grade: 1
Early-Intervention Level: 14

Internet Sites

FactHound offers a safe, fun way to find Internet sites related to this book. All of the sites on FactHound have been researched by our staff.

Here's how:

1. Visit *www.facthound.com*

2. Choose your grade level.

3. Type in this book ID **073686346X** for age-appropriate sites. You may also browse subjects by clicking on letters, or by clicking on pictures and words.

4. Click on the **Fetch It** button.

Facthound will fetch the best sites for you!